D1530377

BEATING BULLYING™

HOW TO BEAT VERBAL BULLYING

LIZ SONNEBORN

rosen publishing's
rosen central®

NEW YORK

Published in 2013 by The Rosen Publishing Group, Inc.
29 East 21st Street, New York, NY 10010

Library of Congress Cataloging-in-Publication Data

Sonneborn, Liz.
How to beat verbal bullying/Liz Sonneborn. — 1st ed.
    p. cm. — (Beating bullying)
Includes bibliographical references and index.
ISBN 978-1-4488-6811-7 (library binding) — ISBN 978-1-4488-6819-3 (pbk.) —
ISBN 978-1-4488-6820-9 (6-pack)
1. Bullying. 2. Verbal self-defense. I. Title.
BF637.B85S66 2013
302.34'3 — dc23

                                                                    2012003926

Manufactured in the United States of America

CPSIA Compliance Information: Batch #S12YA: For further information, contact Rosen Publishing, New York, New York, at 1-800-237-9932.

CONTENTS

According to later reports and investigations, Phoebe Prince began her freshman year at South Hadley High School full of hope. She had recently moved to South Hadley, Massachusetts, from Ireland. The dark-haired girl was lively, pretty, and smart. She dreamed of one day becoming a journalist.

Early in the school year, Prince briefly dated a senior who was a star of the football team. The relationship ended when she found out he had another girlfriend. But the other girl and her friends were still angry at and jealous of Prince. For months, they tormented her at school, calling her the ugliest, cruelest names they could think of, often when other students and teachers were nearby. The abuse didn't stop there. Prince's bullies shoved her into a locker and threatened over and over to beat her up. They also wrote notes on Facebook, telling Prince she should kill herself. Scared of what the bullies might do, she asked her friends to walk with her down the school's halls. But throughout it all, Prince tried to keep her head up and not let the insults and name-calling get to her.

When she first arrived at school on the morning of January 14, 2010, Prince was upbeat. She talked with a friend about how much she was looking forward to an upcoming dance. But soon the bullying began, and on this day, it was relentless. At the school library and in the hallway, her tormentors hissed out nasty remarks and curses. When school let out, as she was walking home, they continued to humiliate her, yelling taunts from a car and throwing an empty drink can at her.

The suicide of Phoebe Prince in 2010 made national news. At school, Prince had been the target of relentless bullying, including verbal insults and threats.

In tears, Prince arrived at her family's house. She found a scarf her sister had given her for Christmas and tied it into a noose. Moments later, she hanged herself. When Phoebe Prince died, she was only fifteen years old.

The suicide of Prince made headlines across the country. People everywhere were shocked by her death and by the abuse she suffered at school. In an unusual step in a bullying case, local prosecutors charged several of her classmates with various crimes. News of the case further infuriated the public when it became clear how little help Prince had received from the teachers and administrators at her high school.

Less commented on was the nature of the bullying Prince endured. She was subjected to some physical bullying. She was also the victim of cyberbullying—a form of harassment in which bullies use the Internet and social media to insult, threaten, and spread rumors about others. But most of Prince's pain came from verbal bullying—name-calling, put-downs, insults, and threats communicated face-to-face. An old adage says, "Sticks and stones may break my bones, but names can never hurt me." However, as Phoebe Prince's story shows, name-calling and other taunts can and do hurt, sometimes so much that victims can feel their lives are worthless.

CHAPTER 1

COPING WITH VERBAL BULLYING

To many teens, bullying means beating someone up. They don't see name-calling and insults as anything unusual or serious. To them, that kind of talk is just part of everyday conversation.

To a degree, they're right. Not every mean remark is an act of verbal bullying. Friends often exchange joking insults with one another. For instance, if a boy gives an embarrassingly wrong answer in class, his friends may make fun of him later, say, by calling him a moron or an idiot. As hurtful as these words may sound, if they're said in a playful way, usually the insulted teen won't take offense. He'll likely counter with a few put-downs of his own, and everyone will end up laughing.

However, the same guy would feel very differently about being called a moron or an idiot by a verbal bully. The bully would say those words hoping to make the victim feel degraded and humiliated. Likely, the bully would try to attract a crowd, making the remarks all the more embarrassing. If the verbal bully went unchallenged, the bully would enjoy a feeling of power over the

Verbal bullies like to draw a crowd when they harass their victims. Having witnesses to the bullying gives them a pleasing sense of power and control.

victim. To get that feeling again, the bully would continue the name-calling over days, weeks, or even months, happily destroying the victim's sense of self-worth.

CHOOSING TARGETS

Verbal bullies are clever in choosing their victims. Like physical bullies, they generally look for people who are weaker than they are. But while bullies who use fists seek out victims who are smaller physically, according to StopBullying.gov, bullies who use words often look for people who have a lower social status. In every school, some students are more popular than others. Verbal bullies often attack their least popular peers because no one is likely to come to their defense.

Often this means verbal bullies pick on teens who are younger and less experienced than they are. For instance, eighth graders may look for sixth graders or new students to harass. Unfamiliar with the school, these students usually don't have many friends yet. They also haven't had the chance to learn who the bullies are and how to avoid them.

Teens who seem unconfident and insecure are also favorite targets. Verbal bullies know that these victims are most likely to take their put-downs and insults to heart. They also lack the confidence to confront a bully or to fight back.

Many verbal bullies reserve their worst scorn for people who have disabilities. Students with disabling conditions, such as muscular dystrophy and cerebral palsy, often suffer abuse. Verbal bullies may perceive being in a wheelchair or just having a stutter as a sign of weakness and therefore an invitation for cruel remarks.

WHEN TEASING HURTS

Say you gained 20 pounds (9 kilograms) in the last year. You've taken to wearing loose shirts, but deep down you know you aren't fooling anyone. Even so, none of your friends have ever said anything about it—except for one. He starts calling you "fatso," "pudge," and "lard butt." Each time he calls you a name, you feel like you want to crawl into a hole and stay there.

Is this verbal bullying? Probably not, but it is teasing that's gone too far. Your friend probably doesn't realize that he's hurting you. The best thing to do is to be straight with him. Tell him that his stupid nicknames make you feel bad about yourself. Probably, that will be enough to make him stop. If it isn't, you'll know that he isn't much of a friend after all.

Students whom others think are odd are also often in trouble. There are a million reasons teens might be labeled as "weird." They might be very shy, speak with a heavy accent, or just laugh too loud at jokes others don't think are funny. Even your clothes can single you out for ridicule. If you dress like a goth when everyone else looks like a prep, verbal bullies might think they can insult and abuse you without other students or even teachers caring.

Occasionally, students are singled out because they possess a special talent. If you're a math whiz or a great singer or a terrific tennis player, you might find other students are jealous of your

New students or students in the lowest grade in a school often become victims of bullies. These students usually haven't made many friends who could help protect them.

achievements. Verbal bullies sometimes decide it's their mission to take you down a notch for the "crime" of distinguishing yourself.

Types of Verbal Attacks

Once verbal bullies choose their victims, they may attack them for just about anything. Most common, though, are insults about the victims' appearance. Bullies might zero in on victims' hair and clothes if they seem at all unusual or out of fashion. They also target people who are overweight or shorter or even taller than most other students their age. Bullies particularly focus on anything about their victims' appearance that might already make them feel insecure, such as having acne on their cheeks or braces on their teeth.

Among younger teens, just having a potentially embarrassing name can attract verbal bullies. You can probably guess that a girl named Jane Butts or a boy named Joe Weiner might have a hard time in middle school. Sometimes, verbal bullies can turn even a perfectly normal name into an insult. For instance, just plain "Jerry" can easily be turned into the taunt "Jerry the Fairy."

As teens get older, sexual bullying becomes more common. Verbal bullies often make rude comments about the developing bodies of their victims, especially if they are girls. However, both boys and girls might come under attack if they don't fit gender stereotypes. For instance, a girl who loves sports and hates skirts might be taunted as a lesbian or a boy who likes fashion and disapproves of violence might be called gay. Sometimes, just being kind or gentle is enough to invite bullies to claim a boy is homosexual.

Similar prejudices encourage verbal bullies to attack people because of their race, ethnicity, or religion. If a student is a member of a minority in the school population, that alone might cause a verbal bully to strike. Bullies assume that if a victim seems different enough, other students will ignore the abuse or perhaps even join in.

Teens who don't fit gender stereotypes are often harassed by their peers. For instance, someone who engages in verbal bullying might think he's insulting a girl who is a great softball player by calling her a lesbian.

RESPONDING TO VERBAL BULLYING

Being the target of a verbal bully is never fun. To even the most self-assured person, cruel words hurt. And effective verbal bullies make sure their words hurt as much as possible. They immediately sense when something they've said gets under their victims' skin. If

An assistant principal comforts students after a school shooting in Tennessee. School shooters sometimes claim that they were verbally bullied by their classmates.

you're sensitive about your weight or embarrassed by your blotchy skin or unsure about your sexual orientation, a verbal bully will hone in on that and figure out just the right words to feed your worst insecurities.

The pain of verbal bullying, however, varies a good deal from person to person. A happy teen with a stable family life may be able to shrug it off. But a troubled or sensitive young person probably can't. Problems that make dealing with bullying more difficult include poverty, neglectful and abusive parents, and depression. Vulnerable teens are likely to feel deep feelings of shame and self-hatred when verbally bullied. Many become so overwhelmed with anxiety that they experience physical effects, such as lack of sleep and headaches and stomachaches. According to *And Words Can Hurt Forever* (2002), the emotional and physical strain of verbal bullying can lead them to make bad decisions that might affect them for the rest of their lives. For instance, middle school students who are bullied might decide to stay home to avoid the bully, which can lead to a gap in learning and in lower grades.

One mistake older teens bullied at school make is to drop out. They come to believe that the only way to deal with their bullies is to steer clear of them completely. But by quitting school, they lose out on educational opportunities, which later limits their ability to find good jobs.

Some bullied teens try to deal with their pain by masking it with drugs and alcohol. These substances provide temporary relief. But all too often, in the long term, their use leads to misery and addiction.

Other bullied young people become so overwhelmed that they lash out in violence. As StopBullying.gov points out, in many recent school shooting cases, the shooters have claimed that they were driven to murder by relentless bullying—often physical bullying, but almost always verbal bullying as well.

Bullying fills other teens with rage that they turn on themselves. Feeling overwhelmed and desperate, some become cutters. Making knife cuts into their own flesh, they feel, at least for a moment, an emotional relief from their stress. Others turn to a more drastic solution. Like Phoebe Prince, they decide that the only way out of their troubles is suicide.

Such tragic responses show how bullied people often blame themselves for the abuse they suffer. But the fault does not lie with them. The real blame always belongs to the bullies, never with their victims.

CHAPTER 2

USING WORDS AS WEAPONS

What makes a person a verbal bully? It may seem like a simple question, but the answer is far from easy to figure out. There are many reasons bullies become bullies. But most verbal bullies at least share a talent for figuring out just the right words to hurt their victims most. Unlike most physical bullies, verbal bullies don't have to be bigger and stronger than the people they attack. They do, though, have to be clever enough with words to make their remarks sting.

CRAVING ATTENTION AND POWER

Deep down, many verbal bullies are looking for one thing—attention. They tend to confront their victims in places where they can easily draw an audience, such as a schoolyard or a locker room. When many teens witness verbal bullying, they disapprove of it but are afraid that, if they say anything, they'll become the next target. But some bystanders enjoy watching bullying. They

Many female bullies prefer to torture their victims with words rather than with fists. Although boys can sometimes earn respect with physical attacks, girls often avoid fighting because they are afraid of being branded as manly.

see bullies as powerful people worthy of respect. At the same time, these witnesses have little sympathy for the victims. They hold the victims in contempt for being unable to defend themselves.

Often verbal bullies face punishment and scorn from adults, such as parents and teachers. But for some, this negative attention is just as satisfying as the positive attention they may receive from their peers. Verbal bullies are frequently desperate for any attention— good or bad—because it makes them feel important. Most teens work to gain status by doing well in class, playing sports, or developing their talent for music, art, writing, or some other interest. Verbal bullies take the easy way, relying on their ability to humiliate and hurt to get recognition from others.

BULLYING AND GENDER

Boys and girls can both be bullies. But, according to *Easing the Teasing*, a book written by Judy S. Freedman, physical bullying is more common among boys. Boys are taught from a young age that being aggressive can earn them respect. Girls, on the other hand, are told that physical fighting is unfeminine. Unlike boys, they are likely to lose status by striking a rival or enemy. As a result, girls often resort to other forms of bullying, including verbal bullying. They use words to attack not just other girls but boys as well. Because they are often physically smaller than boys their same age, female bullies are unlikely to challenge them with fists. However, they may feel comfortable striking out against physically larger but emotionally weaker boys with cruel insults and taunts.

Another thing many verbal bullies crave is a feeling of power. By making their victims seem weak, they feel strong and superior. This feeling is especially appealing to bullies who have a sense of helplessness about everything else going on in their lives.

HURT AND FRUSTRATION

It is also common for verbal bullies to have poor social skills, according to Judy S. Freedman, author of *Easing the Teasing*. They may be very smart and quick, but they feel uncomfortable dealing with other people. That frustration leads them to lash out at their peers. When other teens seem to enjoy their bullying, they are encouraged. Through bullying, they feel they've found a way to relate to their peers and earn their admiration.

Many verbal bullies also have a problem with anger. Often, something in their home life has made them very upset and angry. For instance, they may have a physically or verbally abusive parent, or their mother and father may be going through a divorce. Only by unleashing that pent-up anger by berating and insulting another teen do these bullies feel relief from their very uncomfortable emotions.

Some bullies are overwhelmed by feelings of anger, sometimes because they have been victims of bullying themselves. By taunting their classmates, these bullies are able to release some of their bottled-up rage.

Many bullies are overwhelmed by anger because they themselves were bullied in the past. When teens have been continually insulted and called names, either at home or at school, they become desperate to unleash the pain they feel. Following the example learned from their own bullies, they begin seeking out weaker peers and abuse them in an effort to regain some of the control and dignity they've lost.

BULLYING AND SCHOOL TRADITION

Many verbal bullies are emotionally damaged by hurt, violence, and pain. But some are confident, happy people who are loved at home and respected at school. They often become involved in bullying because they are expected to. For example, some schools have long-standing traditions in which upperclassmen abuse lowerclassmen. This is especially true among members of high school sports teams. Even if the school's teachers and administrators do not actively encourage this behavior, they might turn a blind eye to it.

Popular athletes often hold a privileged position. They are at the top of the high school social order. They are not only held in high regard by other students but also by the faculty. Because star athletes are frequently admired by their teachers, they know they can get away with just about anything, including verbally bullying and sexually harassing any student they choose.

When such verbal bullying is clearly tolerated by a school, athletes, often those of high school age, and other privileged students come to see it almost as an obligation. They think they should pick on younger students or insult anyone who seems different because it is their job to keep the student body in line. After the Columbine school shooting of 1999, in which two students killed twelve of their classmates and one teacher, many news reports mulled over the students' claims that they were driven to their crimes by relentless bullying. As quoted in *And Words Can Hurt Forever*, one Columbine student defended his right to harass other students that don't fit in: "Columbine is a clean, good place except for those rejects. Most kids didn't want them here....Sure, we teased them. But what do you expect with kids who come to school with weird hairdos and horns on their hats? It's not just the jocks; the whole school's disgusted with them....If you want to get rid of someone, usually you tease 'em."

At some schools, not all verbal bullies are students. All too often, teachers who are expected to protect teens from abuse are the worst bullies of all. In class, they might enjoy humiliating students who get an answer wrong. They may make sarcastic comments or yell at them, calling them "stupid" or declaring them

Some of the worst verbal bullies are popular in school. Outstanding athletes, for instance, often become bullies because they are so respected by their classmates and teachers that they feel they can get away with anything.

"losers" in front of their friends and classmates. Coaches may also resort to verbal bullying to punish athletes for losing a game or making a mistake on the playing field. Many of these educators claim that shouting at and insulting students is the only way they can get through to them.

But verbal bullying is never acceptable, whether it is done by a teen or by a teacher, parent, or other authority figure. Luckily, there are strategies that you can use to protect yourself from verbal bullies. And as schools and communities are beginning to take the problem of bullying more seriously, there are also ways you can work with other concerned students and adults to make sure that no one has to endure the shame and pain of a bully's taunts, insults, and name-calling.

MYTHS and FACTS

MYTH Only weaklings and losers are victims of verbal bullying.

FACT Verbal bullies often seek out victims who are feeling insecure and temporarily having trouble fitting in with their peers. Such teens might be upset about something about their home life, embarrassed about natural physical changes in their bodies, or shy around large groups of people. But none of these situations makes these victims weak or bad. It just means they are going through a difficult time, which unfortunately makes them easy prey for verbal bullies looking for someone to hurt.

MYTH All verbal bullies lack self-esteem and self-confidence.

FACT Certainly, some verbal bullies are desperate to win the respect (or fear) of their peers by picking on people they deem as weaker than themselves. But just as often, popular teens use verbal bullying to retain their high status. They can sometimes be the most vicious verbal bullies. Because they are often well liked by other teens and teachers, they know they are unlikely to be punished for harassing other students.

MYTH Verbal bullying is less harmful than physical bullying.

FACT A victim of a physical bully will likely suffer bruises, scrapes, and cuts. But those physical hurts heal with time. The emotional pain felt by victims of verbal bullying, on the other hand, can stay fresh for a far longer period of time. This is especially true when victims are too ashamed to talk about their experiences to ask for support from friends, parents, or other trusted adults.

CHAPTER 3

DEFENDING YOURSELF

If you become the victim of a verbal bully, there are many things you can do to deal with the situation. But no matter what action you take, you should always keep one idea in mind: You are not to blame. The bully, of course, will try to make you feel it's all your fault because you're weaker or whatever. But no matter how upset the bully makes you, do everything you can to remember you've done nothing wrong. The bully deserves to feel shame and embarrassment, not you.

CHALLENGING A BULLY

If a bully begins bothering you, there's one piece of advice you're likely to hear: Just ignore the bully and walk away. Sometimes, walking away can work. Most bullies are hoping to get a reaction out of their victims to confirm that they have hurt them. Refusing to make eye contact and walking off, pretending the bullying didn't even happen, can therefore frustrate some bullies. After a few encounters, they might give up because they aren't getting the feeling of control and power they crave.

Sometimes confronting verbal bullies directly will get them to stand down, especially if the victim rallies friends to lend their support.

But often walking away doesn't end the bullying. Particularly persistent bullies will interpret that as a show of weakness. Or especially frustrated bullies may decide, if words aren't working, it's time to pull out their fists. Also, sometimes, walking away is impossible. If you're on a school bus, for instance, you are stuck listening to your bully's taunts until you reach your stop.

Depending on the situation, you can also try confronting a verbal bully. Just telling a bully in no uncertain terms to cut it out might end the problem. If you can manage to make a joke at the bully's expense, all the better. These strategies, however, usually work only if you have plenty of friends around to support you.

Another strategy is to dismiss the bully's comments, as though they aren't worth your time. A response of "So what?" or "Big deal" or "Whatever" can make bullies look stupid, especially if they aren't quick with a comeback. You might also try agreeing with a bully to put the bully off guard. If a bully starts harping on your weight, for instance, you could say, "Yeah, I could stand to lose a few pounds. Thanks so much for pointing that out." The bully might not be prepared with another insult, giving you a chance to get away. Or you could bluntly say that you don't care what a bully thinks. If a bully insults your appearance, you could stand up straight, look the bully in the eye, and say, "I like how I look." Such a straightforward approach can make you seem much more powerful than your bully.

CHANGING YOUR BEHAVIOR

Confronting a bully is not easy for a lot of teens. Some are so shy or insecure that they'd never feel comfortable doing that. However, even in that case, there are still plenty of things victims can do.

Imagine you have a bully who attacks at the same time in the same place every day. Try changing your routine. If you can't, talk to your friends and ask them to stay near you when the bully is around. If you're surrounded by friends, the bully may stop thinking of you as an easy target.

If your bully used to be your friend, try to figure out why he or she suddenly decided to pick on you. Maybe you accidentally hurt the person or somehow made him or her envious of you. It may be worth trying to talk it out with your bully. If you can find out why the bully is so upset, you can either apologize or explain your side of things.

If a bully attacks you because of how you dress or because you make good grades, you may think new clothes or a flunking grade will end the abuse. In most cases, though, it won't. If you seem like a good victim, the bully will just find something else about you to

If a verbal bully attacks you at the same place and time every day, ask your friends to stay close to you when you expect the bully to be around. As they say, there's safety in numbers.

make fun of. But in some cases, bullies decide that it's their duty to deride a person about a particularly annoying habit or behavior. For instance, if a bully taunts you for talking too loud or for having bad breath, you might ask your friends if there's something to the charge. If there is, you might want to work on speaking in a normal tone of voice or brushing your teeth more often. Working to change a bad habit may or may not get a bully off your back, but it may make your dealings with other people better.

Even though it's painful, spend a moment thinking about how you respond when a verbal bully picks on you. Do you cry or put your head down, slump your shoulders, and stare at the ground? If you do, you are playing right into your bully's hands. Working to get

Even if you feel insecure, try holding your head up and shoulders back. By looking self-confident, you may be able to discourage verbal bullies, who are always on the lookout for victims with little self-esteem.

better control of your emotions and shyness may therefore discourage the bullying. Even if you don't feel self-confident, try to look like you do. Just carrying yourself with your head up and shoulders back will make you feel better. It will also send the message that you are a person deserving of respect. To feel better about yourself, you may also want to spend more time on activities you're good at and enjoy. Even if a bully is trying to drag you down, you can pull yourself up by exploring your talents and remembering your accomplishments.

Just as there are positive ways of dealing with verbal bullying, there are also negative strategies that will only serve to hurt you. For instance, try to resist hitting your bully. Escalating a case of verbal bullying into a physical fight usually makes the situation worse in the long run. Also, if teachers or parents get involved, they'll likely blame and punish you for striking the first blow.

You might be tempted to protect yourself by joining a gang. But that can easily backfire by getting you involved in a violent world you can't easily get out of. If you're a girl who's tired of sexual remarks from a verbal bully, you might get into a romantic relationship with the biggest, physically most menacing boy you know. That may

WITNESSING VERBAL BULLYING

The victim is not the only person who gets hurt by verbal bullying. Anyone who witnesses an act of verbal bullying is likely to be affected as well. Many witnesses want to tell the bullies to stop but feel too frightened. They are convinced that if they speak up, they'll become the next target. Afterward, they feel guilty that they stood by silently, especially if the victim is a friend. When adults take no action against bullies, witnesses also begin to feel unsafe. If bullies can do whatever they want without punishment, they ask themselves, what's to stop them from attacking me next time?

make you feel safer, but it's not fair to you (or him) to get into a relationship where there's no real affection.

ASKING FOR HELP

Understand, though, that sometimes it is nearly impossible to solve a bullying problem on your own. If you feel overwhelmed by a verbal bully, you need to tell someone about what's been happening to you. Try talking to a close friend or two if you're uncomfortable talking with an adult. Your friends may not be able to stop the bullying. But just talking about it will probably make you feel less alone and better able to handle the situation.

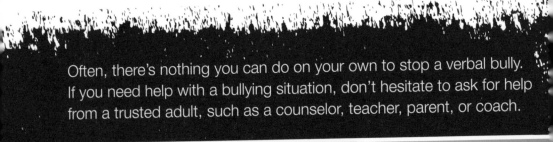

Often, there's nothing you can do on your own to stop a verbal bully. If you need help with a bullying situation, don't hesitate to ask for help from a trusted adult, such as a counselor, teacher, parent, or coach.

When you're ready to talk to an adult, choose someone you know and trust. That can be a parent, another relative, an older friend, a neighbor, a teacher, a coach, a principal, a counselor, or a school nurse. Some schools have antibullying policies in place, with specific employees trained in helping bully victims. If you don't know if your school has such a policy, a favorite teacher will probably know or be able to find out.

Even a caring adult might try to downplay your troubles with verbal bullying. If you get this reaction, don't give up. Tell another adult who might be more understanding. If your friends have witnessed the bullying, ask for their help. Bring them with you to back you up when you tell your story. Together, you may be able to persuade your school and community to finally get serious about verbal bullying.

10 GREAT QUESTIONS
to Ask a Guidance Counselor

1 What is verbal bullying?

2 Is there a difference between verbal bullying and teasing?

3 Why do people become verbal bullies?

4 How do verbal bullies choose their targets?

5 How does verbal bullying affect its victims?

6 Who should teens tell if they are being verbally bullied?

7 What should teens do if they witness verbal bullying?

8 What are schools doing to curb verbal bullying?

9 Are there laws against verbal bullying?

10 Are there any organizations that help teens who are hurt by verbal bullying?

CHAPTER 4

FIGHTING BACK

Sadly, Phoebe Prince is not the only verbal bullying victim to make news in recent years. Chris Joyner, Brian Head, Tyler Clementi, and Jamey Rodemeyer are just a few of the many other teenagers who have been driven to suicide by bullying behavior. These high-profile cases have had a huge impact across the United States. They've forced millions of parents and educators to reexamine their ideas about verbal bullying. At the same time, they've compelled communities to come up with new strategies to end bullying once and for all.

ANTIBULLYING PROGRAMS

Even as antibullying measures are becoming more popular, many adults continue to resist them. Some parents think bullying, especially verbal bullying, is a normal part of growing up. They think their kids need to learn to stand up for themselves when threatened and to develop a thick-enough skin that bullies' insults won't hurt them. In some cases, effectively dealing with

▶ **What's New!**
  click here

▶ **NCSE Approach
to School Success**

**Attendance
Attachment
Achievement**

**NCSE Tools for
School Success**

- **Bully Proof Your
School**

  BPYS is an essential tool to
  improve school climate,
  address bystander and
  bullying behavior and create

Bully Proof Your School

Summary & Information

Numerous studies report that many children across the nation are fearful in their schools and in their neighborhoods. This fear is not only due to the more extreme forms of school violence that have been reported in the media, but to the high incidence of bullying and harassment that takes place daily in U.S. schools. *Bully-Proofing Your School* (BPYS) is a nationally recognized school safety program, implemented in school districts throughout the United States and Canada, with a scientifically proven track record since its inception in 1992. BPYS is a critical element in the creation of safe, civil and caring school culture that, in turn, promotes student attachment to school, attendance at school and achievement in school.

Why Does Bullying Matter?
The 1993 National Household Education Survey, based on the responses of 6,504

The National Center for School Engagement (http://www.schoolengagement .org) has developed the Bully Proof Your School program. This program helps schools throughout the United States and Canada create a safe and bully-free environment for their students.

---

a bully can build self-confidence. But much more often, verbal bullying makes young people feel less confident, not only in their teen years but also long into adulthood.

Schools, too, are often slow to address bullying issues. Sometimes, the school staff just doesn't know how bad the bullying is because students are reluctant to report it. In other schools, administrators purposely downplay bullying because they don't want to be seen as doing a bad job. Also, teachers frequently don't want to deal with a verbal bullying problem. They think their job is to teach classes, not to police students' conversations with each other.

VERBAL BULLYING AND U.S. LAW

Some U.S. laws address certain extreme cases of verbal bullying in public schools. For instance, discrimination is prohibited on the basis of race, color, and national origin (Civil Rights Act of 1964), on the basis of gender (Education Amendments of 1972), and on the basis of disability (Americans with Disabilities Act of 1990). If a school is taken to court and found to have an overly hostile atmosphere because of any of these forms of discrimination, it can lose its funding from the federal government. However, students suffering from verbal harassment based on other differences, such as sexual orientation, now have no recourse under federal law. For this reason, some antibullying experts support the Student Non-Discrimination Act, which is being considered by the U.S. Congress. It would prohibit any bullying, including verbal harassment against lesbian, gay, bisexual or transgender (LGBT) teens.

The majority of school employees, though, do understand that they have a responsibility to keep students safe. To keep weapons out of schools and to monitor student interaction, many schools have installed metal detectors and surveillance cameras. While these measures may reduce violent interactions, they create an atmosphere of fear that can interfere with learning. They also do little to prevent or address the emotional troubles students suffer from nonphysical forms of bullying.

For this reason, some schools are now adopting more comprehensive antibullying programs. The Olweus Program, Steps to Respect, and Bully Proof Your School are just a few of the most popular of these. Generally antibullying programs encourage students to talk about bullying and give them concrete ways as victims and as bystanders to deal with the problem. They encourage everyone to report instances of bullying, no matter how minor, and often train certain teachers and school staff members as bullying experts. Antibullying programs also try to teach students to respect differences in their classmates and to develop sympathy for bullying victims.

LEGAL MEASURES

Many schools have adopted antibullying policies on their own. But others have done so in response to state laws that seek to end child and teen bullying in public schools. Since 1999, all states except for three (North Dakota, South Dakota, and Hawaii) have adopted some type of antibullying law. The most sweeping legislation was passed in New Jersey in 2010 after a year of consultation with some of the country's leading experts in bullying. The law addresses

Michigan lawmakers celebrate after Governor Rich Snyder signs an antibullying bill into law in 2011. The law requires school districts across the state to take specific steps to discourage and deal with bullying.

bullying committed both on and off school grounds and establishes a Week of Respect early in the school year, during which students are instructed in how to prevent physical confrontations and harassment. Unlike some antibullying laws, it takes verbal bullying as seriously as physical bullying.

There is no national antibullying law, but the federal government has recently addressed the bullying problem by establishing an annual Federal Partners in Bullying Prevention Summit. In September 2011, the second bullying summit brought together 175 experts from schools, government agencies, and nonprofit organizations to develop a national antibullying strategy. To spread information about bullying developed during these conferences, the Department of Health and Human Services established the StopBullying.gov Web site.

ANTIBULLYING ORGANIZATIONS

Many private organizations are also working to educate the public about bullying. For instance, the PACER Center, a group that supports parents of children with disabilities, promotes antibullying programs through its Bullying Prevention Center in Minneapolis, Minnesota. Since 2006, the center has asked individuals and communities to observe October as National Bullying Prevention Month. As part of this event, the organization encourages students on October 12 to participate in Unity Day, whose slogan is "Make It Orange and Make It End." To show support for bullying victims, students wear orange clothing and pass out orange unity ribbons at their schools.

Another antibullying organization was founded by two young adult novelists, Carrie Jones and Megan Kelley Hall. Shocked by the suicide of Phoebe Prince, they established the Facebook page Young Adult Authors Against Bullying. There, fellow writers shared their own stories of being bullied as a way of comforting and showing

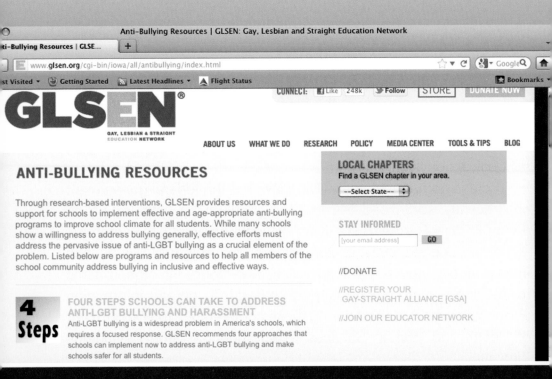

support for teen victims. In 2011, many of these stories were collected into the book *Dear Bully: 70 Authors Tell Their Stories* and on the Web site DearBully.com.

Most antibullying efforts deal with various types of bullying. But GLSEN (Gay, Lesbian & Straight Education Network) established No Name-Calling Week specifically to draw attention to verbal bullying. Promoted with the slogan "No sticks, no stones, no dissing," No Name-Calling Week each year encourages schools and communities to sponsor educational activities designed to stop harmful and hurtful name-calling among young people.

JOINING THE FIGHT

All of these various campaigns against bullying have made parents, teachers, and students more aware of the issue. But no antibullying program can accomplish much without the involvement of teens like you. After all, you are on the frontlines of teen bullying. Even if you haven't been bullied, you have likely seen it happening to someone else. Teachers and other caring adults, however, may not be aware of exactly what's happening to you and your friends and classmates. If you want to see bullying come to an end, you have to speak out and tell them what you know.

But your responsibility doesn't end there. You need to make sure that adults understand that bullying is about more than physical violence. Many adults were raised in a time when most people thought being called names was just a normal part of growing up. But research shows that's wrong. Verbal bullying is damaging to everyone—both to those who hear the words and to those who say them.

If you're a verbal bully, stop what you're doing. If you're the victim of verbal bullying, tell someone and ask for help. And if you're a witness to verbal bullying, report it and support the victim. No matter what your experience, remember that putting an end to verbal bullying starts with you.

GLOSSARY

cyberbullying A type of bullying in which bullies use the Internet and social media to insult, threaten, and spread rumors about others.

discrimination Unjust treatment inflicted on people because they belong to a certain group, such as a race, religion, or gender.

ethnicity The state of belonging to a group distinguished by shared national origins.

gay A person (especially a man) who is sexually attracted to those of the person's own gender.

gender The state of being female or male.

harass To bother, intimidate, or pressure.

lesbian A woman who is sexually attracted to other women.

LGBT Lesbian, gay, bisexual, or transgender.

prejudice A preconceived judgment about a person or thing not based on actual experience or facts.

self-esteem Self-respect and confidence in one's abilities.

sexual orientation A sexual attraction to one or both genders.

social media Online tools that allow users to communicate with one another.

status A person's social standing in relation to others in a group.

stereotype A widely held but oversimplified or incorrect view of a group of people.

taunt A remark made to anger or upset someone.

teasing Name-calling and insulting language meant to make playful fun of another.

verbal bullying A type of bullying that employs name-calling, insults, and cruel remarks.

vicious Deliberately cruel or violent.

vulnerable Capable of easily being hurt.

BullyingCanada
471 Smythe Street
P.O. Box 27009
Fredericton, NB E3B 9M1
Canada
(877) 352-4497
Web site: http://www.bullyingcanada.ca
This organization offers support for bullied young people through-
    out Canada.

GLSEN
90 Broad Street, 2nd Floor
New York, NY 10004
(212) 727-0135
Web site: http://www.glsen.org
GLSEN (Gay, Lesbian & Straight Education Network) works to
    protect all students from harassment and bullying. It addresses
    verbal bullying by sponsoring the annual No Name-Calling
    Week program.

Office of Safe and Healthy Students
Office of Elementary and Secondary Education
400 Maryland Avenue SW
Washington, DC 20202
(202) 401-0113
Web site: http://www2.ed.gov/about/offices/list/oese/index.html
This office of the federal government works to keep schools safe
    through programs that promote violence prevention and char-
    acter education.

Olweus Bullying Prevention Program
Institute on Family & Neighborhood Life
Clemson University
158 Poole Agricultural Center
Clemson, SC 29634
(864) 656- 6712
Web site: http://www.clemson.edu/olweus
Used in thousands of American schools, the Olweus Program
provides instruction for preventing bullying and improving
relations between students.

PACER's National Bullying Prevention Center
8161 Normandale Boulevard
Bloomington, MN 55437
(888) 248-0822
Web site: http://www.pacer.org/bullying
Founder of the National Bullying Prevention Month, PACER
educates communities in how to prevent and address all
forms of bullying.

StopBullying.gov
U.S. Department of Health and Human Services
200 Independence Avenue SW
Washington, DC 20201
Web site: http://www.stopbullying.gov
This Web site provides age-appropriate materials for young
people, parents, and teachers about how to understand
and stop bullying.

HOTLINES

Boys Town National Hotline (800) 448-3000

Covenant House Youth Crisis Hotline (800) 999-9999

CrisisLink (888) 644-5886

Kids Help Phone Canada (800) 668-6868

National Suicide Hotline (800) 784-2433

National Suicide Prevention Lifeline (800) 273-TALK
    or (800) 273-8255

TEEN LINE (800) 852-8336

Trevor Project Hotline (866) 4-U-TREVOR or (866) 488-7386

WEB SITES

Due to the changing nature of Internet links, Rosen Publishing has developed an online list of Web sites related to the subject of this book. This site is updated regularly. Please use this link to access the list:

http://www.rosenlinks.com/beat/verb

FOR FURTHER READING

Belleza, Rhoda, ed. *Cornered: 13+ Stories About Bullying*. Philadelphia, PA: Running Press Kids, 2012.

Ellis, Deborah. *We Want You to Know: Kids Talk About Bullying*. Custer, WA: Coteau Books, 2010.

Guillain, Charlotte. *Coping with Bullying*. Chicago, IL: Heinemann-Raintree, 2011.

Hall, Megan Kelley, and Carrie Jones, eds. *Dear Bully: 70 Authors Tell Their Stories*. New York, NY: HarperTeen, 2011.

Preller, James. *Bystander*. New York, NY: Feiwel & Friends, 2009.

Shapiro, Ouisie. *Bullying and Me: Schoolyard Stories*. Chicago, IL: Albert Whitman & Company, 2010.

Sprague, Susan. *Coping with Cliques: A Workbook to Help Girls Deal with Gossip, Put-Downs, Bullying and Other Mean Behavior*. 2nd ed. Oakland, CA: Instant Help Books, 2008.

Tarshis, Thomas Paul. *Living with Peer Pressure and Bullying*. New York, NY: Facts On File, 2010.

Withers, Jennie, with Phyllis Hendrickson. *Hey, Back Off! Tips for Stopping Teen Harassment*. Far Hills, NJ: New Horizons Press, 2011.

BIBLIOGRAPHY

Breakstone, Steve, Michael Dreiblatt, and Karen Dreiblatt. *How to Stop Bullying and Social Aggression*. Thousand Oaks, CA: Corwin Press, 2008.

Coloroso, Barbara. *The Bully, the Bullied, and the Bystander*. New York, NY: HarperResource, 2003.

Espelage, Dorothy L., and Susan M. Swearer, eds. *Bullying in North American Schools*. 2nd ed. New York, NY: Routledge, 2010.

Field, Julaine E., Jered B. Kolbert, Laura M. Crothers, and Tammy L. Hughes, eds. *Understanding Girl Bullying and What to Do About It*. Thousand Oaks, CA: Corwin Press, 2009.

Freedman, Judy S. *Easing the Teasing: Helping Your Child Cope with Name-Calling, Ridicule, and Verbal Bullying*. Chicago, IL: Contemporary Books, 2002.

Fried, SuEllen, and Blanche Sosland. *Banishing Bullying Behavior: Transforming the Culture of Pain, Rage, and Revenge*. Lanham, MD: Rowman & Littlefield Education, 2009.

Garbarino, James, and Ellen deLara. *And Words Can Hurt Forever: How to Protect Adolescents from Bullying, Harassment, and Emotional Violence*. New York, NY: Free Press, 2002.

Guerin, Suzanne, and Eilis Hennessey. *Aggression and Bullying*. Malden, MA: Wiley-Blackwell, 2011.

Haber, Joel, with Jenna Glatzer. *Bullyproof Your Child for Life: Protect Your Child from Teasing, Taunting, and Bullying for Good*. New York, NY: Perigee, 2007.

Pickhardt, Carl. *Why Good Kids Act Cruel: The Hidden Truth About the Pre-Teen Years*. Naperville, IL: Sourcebooks, 2010.

Rivers, Ian. *Homophobic Bullying: Research and Theoretical Perspectives*. New York, NY: Oxford University Press, 2011.

Roberts, Walter B., Jr. *Bullying from Both Sides: Strategic Interventions for Working with Bullies and Victims*. Thousand Oaks, CA: Corwin Press, 2006.

Sullivan, Keith, et al. *Bullying in Secondary Schools: What It Looks Like and How to Manage It*. Thousand Oaks, CA: Corwin Press, 2004.

Urbanski, Jan, and Steve Permuth. *The Truth About Bullying: What Educators and Parents Must Know and Do*. Lanham, MD: Rowman & Littlefield Education, 2009.

INDEX

ABOUT THE AUTHOR

Liz Sonneborn is a writer living in Brooklyn, New York. A graduate of Swarthmore College, she is the author of more than eighty books for children, young adults, and adult readers. Sonneborn's books about teen issues include *Treating Obesity*, *Frequently Asked Questions About Plagiarism*, and *Frequently Asked Questions About Shoplifting and Theft*.

PHOTO CREDITS